LAWET

WHEN LAWYER BECOMES POET

KAUSTAV GHOSH

Copyright © Kaustav Ghosh
All Rights Reserved.

This book has been published with all efforts taken to make the material error-free after the consent of the author. However, the author and the publisher do not assume and hereby disclaim any liability to any party for any loss, damage, or disruption caused by errors or omissions, whether such errors or omissions result from negligence, accident, or any other cause.

While every effort has been made to avoid any mistake or omission, this publication is being sold on the condition and understanding that neither the author nor the publishers or printers would be liable in any manner to any person by reason of any mistake or omission in this publication or for any action taken or omitted to be taken or advice rendered or accepted on the basis of this work. For any defect in printing or binding the publishers will be liable only to replace the defective copy by another copy of this work then available.

I dedicate this book to my family members; especially my parents and elder sister. They have been my source of energy and motivation throughout my life. Without their support, my life would have been dark as the sky of the night.

Contents

Contents

Contents

Foreword

Lawet means law, poetry, and more. Learning new things has been my passion since my childhood. So I started lawet.in for learning, relearning, and unlearning several things and want to share it with the world. My dream is to make this World free from racism, hatred, and violence so that my future generation can live peacefully. But I all alone cannot make this world beautiful and safe, but together we can achieve any object. That's why say I say I can't, you can't, but together we all can. Lawet- A lawyer becomes a poet.

Preface

LAWET started its journey in February 2022. But it all started while I was writing my first poetry book '**A Bengali Patriot**' in the year 2021. On the cover page, I mentioned the name '**LAWET**' first, which means **LAWYER+POET. LAWET** started its journey on as a podcasting channel and soon it become a blogging website. Lawet.in become the platform to showcase my legal and poetry skill. Now it needs your blessing. I, Kaustav Ghosh, humbly solicit your review so that it becomes bigger and better. This poetry books consists of 50 poems. They have different flavour. They are waiting for you.

1. Story of Lawet

কেমিস্টির্র বই গুলো ছিল আমার কাছে কবিতার মত।

ঠিক পর্থম পের্ম যেমন হয়।

অ্গরানিক বা ইন অ্গরানিক, যেন এক একটা ছন্দ।

জানি না কবে থেকে তোকে ভালবেসে ফেলে ছিলাম।

সেটা ক্লাস সিক্স সেভেন ছিল কিনা।

সবে গোঁফ গজিয়েছে, ঝড় ঝঞ্জার কালে পদা্পরণ।

কেমিস্টির্র সাথে যেন সাহিত্য সৃষ্টি করতে নেমেছিলাম আমি।

পেরেছিলাম কেমিস্টির্র সাথে আলাদা কেমিস্টির্ থাকার জন্য়।

অঙ্কর সাথে অঙ্ক মেলাতে না পের্রে;

কেমিস্টির্ কেই করে ফেললাম জীবনের সব কিছু।

রচনা করে ফেললাম যৌগ, মৌল, ধাতু নিয়ে কবিতা।

জীবন কিভাবে এগোবে সর্বকিছুই যেন পরিষ্কার দেখতে পাচ্ছিলাম নিজের তৈরী গবেষণাগার থেকে।

এগিয়ে যাব নিজের ভালবাসা নিয়ে।

আসলে খুব বোকা ছিলাম, খুব ই।

পরাইমারি থেকে যাদের সাথে জীবন এর এই যাতর়া টা শুরু করেছিলাম,

তারা কবে ফেলে চলে গেছে নিজেদের গন্তবেয়।

বুঝতেই পারি নি সেটা।

আসলে কথা তো অন্য় রকম ছিল।

কথা তো ছিল একসাথে ওই বাসে ওঠা,
গন্তবয় যে আলাদা ভাবিনি কখনো।

জানিস মন, ওদের কাউকে কখন ও কাঁদতে দি নি।

তাই ভাবি নি কেউ আমার চোখের জল দেখে-

এত খুশী হবে, এতটা খুশী।

ওদের কে এই জলটাই উপহার দিয়ে ছিলাম।

তারপর এলো একটা ঝড়।

অবাক হয়ে দেখলাম কেমিস্টির্ ও জীবন থেকে চলে গেল।

ধব্বংস হয়ে গেল গবেষনা,

পুড়ে ছাই হয়ে গেল কবিতার খাতা।

এবার সবাই খুশী, কারণ ওরা ভেবেছিল আমি শেষ।

ওরা আমাকে চেনেই নি, আসলে চেনার চেষ্টাই করে নে।

চিনলে জানতে পারতো সেই ফুলটি কে।

যে ধব্বংসস্তূপ থেকে বারবার জন্ম নেয়।

সে জন্ম নিল সাদা জামা কালো কোটির পরে।

নতুন রূপে নতুন ভাবে-

সওয়াল জবাব করতে নয়ায়ের হয়ে।

অবিচারের বিরুদ্ধ জারি তার বজর্নিঘেরাষ।

সে বদলে গেলেও সে আগের মত আজ ও চায় তাই-

মন খুলে হাসুক আর পরাণ ভরে বাঁচুক সব্বাই।

Chapter2

কবিতা-

শুধু কি কত গুলো কথা??

অথবা কতগুলো লাইন।

নাকি কিছু শব্দ দিয়ে ছান্দিক কারুকায্যর।

নাকি কবির মনের মাধুরী মিশিয়ে তৈরী হয় অননয় এক শিল্প।

কবিতা কি শুধু ছন্দময় এক সৃষ্টি।

নাকি তার চেয়েও বেশী কিছু।

কবিতা তো ভাবনার এক নাম-

জীনর যে পুরাতন তা মুছে নতুন কে আহব্বান।

সেই আহব্বান মন্তর্ই তো কবিতা।

কবিতার মাধয্ম দিয়ে হয় নতুন কিছুর শুরু।

আদ্শর কে এগিয়ে নিয়ে যাওয়ার গন মাধযম।

কবিতা মনের কথা গুলো কত সুন্দর ভাবে ফুটিয়ে তোলে।

মনের অনুভূতি গুলো আরো পর্জব্বলিত হয়ে ওঠে।

জীবন নতুন মানে পায় এই কবিতার হাত ধরে।

3. I will Rise

I will rise from the ashes,

I will rise from the scratches.

I will rise even after none know my worth today,

I will rise like have risen up already.

I may not rise in a day,

May not have rise today.

But one day I will rise-

I will rise like no one else.

I will rise from the demented hell,

I will rise like have risen up already.

I will rise from the street corner,

I will rise from the heart of the people.

I will rise from the every gossip,

I will rise from the every mocking they make.

I will rise even after they shame on my body, my looks.

I will my rise even after they hate my language, my ethnicity,

my color.

I will rise after every failure.

I will rise after every heart break, betrayal.

I will rise after every burn,

I will rise, I will shine like the Sun

4. Durgapuja- The festival of Homecoming

Durga puja- The festival of four days.

The festival we wait for 360 days for that four days.

The festival of forgetting all the pain, loss, and failure.

The festival to re-energised yourself.

But you may ask why its the festival of homecoming?

Many people travel outside this time.

May be they are finding home outside home?

For a change or for getting some new flavor.

Flavor of life.

Now about home coming.

I found it, I found it.

The secret to happiness.

The happiness of durga puja.

Bengalis-

Mostly god loving, less god fearing.

We think god is dearer than dearest.

This is why Durga become daughter from goddess.

A daughter comes to his parent after marriage.

Be it four days or one.

When she comes,

Specially after marriage, long time no meeting.

Yes, I can feel it.

Yes, I can feel the joy.
I can feel the happiness.
Specially after my sister's marriage-
When she comes after longtime.
I smell the essence of Durga puja.
I can feel the same happiness.
Maybe this is what Durga puja is all about-
To find Durga in every daughter.
Durga puja-not only the homecoming of the holy mother.
But also the home coming of every soul from dust.

5. True Friendship

When none was there,
You hold my hands like none other even think of.
When even my shadow moves into another,
You stay there.
Like an ever-lasting friendship.
You are there to talk when none was there to speak.
Yes, when none was there to speak-
Either speak for me or with me.
When there was cheating, betrayal and heart break;
When I could not trust myself,
I shared everything with you.
You listen to me, you heard me.
With the patience of billions of years.
Still I could not choose you for eternity.
Still I could not see you,
Still I search for human who can be seen.
Even after you make me realise you hear, you can be seen.
I forget that, oh dear I forget that.
I forget diamonds while search for gold.
I forget that self interest is the key which make people around you.
Forgive me my dear, forgive my weakness.
Its a promise to you I will wait-

Will wait for you till my last day.
Will wait for you till I got the salvation.
You will be in me, I will be in you.

6. 'L' STORY

All starts with 'A', even the word 'All' .

But in my life all starts with 'L'.

Wait a minute!

Even 'life' starts with 'L'

Lets look back to my life.

Love was the first feelings,

Which I had.

Which I could understand when I understood nothing.

Love at first sight they said-

It happened, it happened for my mother.

'Love starts with 'L'-

It all started with 'L'.

In fact it all started with 'A' also-

'Ashapurna' my mother.

'Ashapurna'-who fulfill all the hopes,

As the meaning goes.

As I started growing I could understand

'L' will not stop with 'ove'.

This time 'L' will take 'ike' with it for the study.

Thanks to the 'like';

I could find feelings for the literature while studying.

Like I have said-

Found 'l' for 'love' for the l for 'literature'.

It all started with 'L'.

I started writing poetry, was not worthy to showcase it.

But have never stop trying.

Quit never an option, it never was.

Improving everyday, only that's matter.

Day after day gone,

I found passion for chemistry in my high school.

So started writing poetry on H2 SO4,

Found an organic bond between me and chemistry.

But still-

I found something was missing.

Took law for graduation,

Though I never ever thought to become an advocate like my father.

Maybe it was in my blood.

From my great grandfather to my father,

Everyone had an affinity for literature.

Choosing L for 'law' seems to be my best decision.

Found l for love of my l for life for law..

Here arises many question.

Why 'l', 'l', so many 'l'??

Not only because 'L' connects many thing.

Like the literature re(l)ates with law.

As they complete and compliment each other.

As the literature helped me to plead before court of law.

As I feel 'law' is the magic created by 'literature'.

No, that is not the reason-

Not the reason for so many 'l' in this poetry and in my 'life'.

'L' decides and directs, 'L' stands for redemption

'L' which stands for 'Luck' will not stand for you if you have loads of laziness.

Laziness will ensure lots of losses.

If you can learn from losses you will lead..

This is the first thing as a lawyer I was introduced.

I have learned to learn, relearn and unlearn.

Learning from mistakes and not repeating it.

Learning everyday, every time, everywhere.

Even you starts earning when you add 'L' to it.

Is not it like an umbrella?

Irrespective of you are 'loser' or 'lucky' 'l' stands with you.

Like the word 'loyalty' for which 'l' stands for.

And here is the magic.

Every word starts with a letter and the word 'letter' starts with 'l'.

But It is the 'l' for 'language.

When there is no 'language' there is no life in letter and literature.

Even life is lifeless without language.

But the fact is everything perished, nothing lasts forever.

Even law repealed, language vanished so as the literature.

Here lies the magic of 'L'

That is 'l' for learning.

Which never perished-

in life and after life.

Learning means you have not given up.

7. মধ্যবিত্ত এবং স্বপ্ন

স্বপ্নগুলো বুঝি মধ্যবিত্ত দের চোখেই ভেসে ওঠে-
গরীব দের তো স্বপ্ন দেখাই মানা।
আর উচ্চবিত্তদের-
তাদের জীবনটাই তো স্বপ্নময়।
শুরু সবাই শূন্য থেকেই করে।
মহাসিন্ধুর ওপার থেকে এসে তার একটাই হয় কাজ-
শূন্যের আগে সংখ্যা বসাতে বসাতে মহাশূন্যের উদ্দেশ্যে যাত্রা।
শূন্য থেকে শুরু করে শেষটা ও যেন শূন্য না হয়।
সমস্যা টা এক; তার সমাধান টা খুব আলাদা কিছু না।
বিত্ত বড় হয়ে নিজের বৃত্ত টা ও বড় রাখা।

8. Kalu the King

It is the story of my Kalu-
For others he may be just a stray dog.
For me, he is the KING KALU.
The cutest and the most obedient I have ever seen.
He is the KING, always a KING.
He roams like KING, sits like the KING.
He rules in our life like none have ever ruled it.
It is the story of him-
He was roaming here and there.
Confused, afraid, traumatized.
He was abandoned by his owner.
My father called him, gave the name 'KALU'.
But I had so many fears for them then.
You came, you took away all that fear I had for dogs.
You came, saw, you won our hearts.
You came to conquer.
You conquer my heart, my everything.
It is my pray to God-
You may have long life and sound health.
For me there is none like Kalu.
Your smile that matters.

9. Waking up from an Indian dream

Waking up from an Indian dream,

A dream that made me awake,

A dream that gift me restless night.

A dream for which I live,

A dream for which I can die.

India, a nation of big dreams-

A nation with so many differences.

India, a nation of tolerance and compassion-

A nation who taught non-violence can be weapon.

From its geography to its culture-

We have not let language to be our barrier.

India, a land of diversity-

Where rich tradition blends with history.

But still it is a nation-

"A union of states".

We could not constitute a country.

Where people will not impose its language, religion and belief.

Where people will not tell you its not your native place.

Where people will not question your nationality here and there.

When there will be no hatred towards differences.

When we would understand this differences make us unique.

You may read many negatives about this nation-
You may find violence, riot, intolerance.
You may watch news on price rise, crisis, unemployment.
India, still a land of dreams.
Why? What may be the reasons?
A dream, daring or nightmare??
It is the 458 million of youths
With the abundance of daring,
With the magical innovations,
With the thinking which none have ever thought of,
With the fire of revolutions in the heart.
It is for the youth I dare to dream,
It is the youth who can fight with nothing.
It is for them our fight is on,
It is for them the dreams are sown.
A dream to make this nation as a country-
A country with zero suicide among youth;
A country with no barrier for love;
A country with religions harmony and mutual respect;
A country with no hatred for language, caste and sect;
Where people will not die for food, cloth and shelter,
A country where mental health will get full attention.
Sounds like mission Impossible??
No, this will come true oneday.
WE WILL MAKE IT COME TRUE.
I have believe instilled in me,
For me and for all the youth.

Together we can create magic.
The dream of all the freedom fighters,
Together we will make it true.
WE WILL, WE WILL, WE WILL.

Chapter10

আমি চাই এক আত্মহত্যাহীন পৃথিবী,
আমি সব্প্ন বুনি সেই পৃথিবীর।
হয়তো আজকের হিসাবে তা আকাশকুসুম।
হয়তো আজকের হিসাবে তা অবাস্তব।
কিন্তু সব্প্ন দেখেই তো যাত্রা শুরু করে বাস্তবের কাহিনী
গুলো,
যে কাহিনী গুলো গল্প হলেও সতিয়।
যেভাবে কুমারটুলির বুকে সৃষ্টি হয় পর্তিমা,
যেভাবে সব্প্নকে বিজ্ঞানীরা করে তোলে বাস্তব,
যে ভাবে সবাধীনতার সব্প্ন দেখে পর্তিটা বিপ্লবী।
বিপ্লবটা কি একটি সব্প্ন নয়?
যে সব্প্নে মানুষ নব উদয়মে বেরিয়ে আসে,
সব্প্ন দিয়েই সবকিছুই হয় শুরু;
যে সব্প্ন দেখেই মানুষ পরিব্তরনের দেয় ডাক।
আমিও তাই সব্প্ন দেখি এক আত্মহত্যাহীন পৃথিবীর।
পাখীরাও হারের আগে মানে না হার,
যদি পশুরা নিজেদের না করে শেষ,
কীটপতঙ্গরাও মরার আগে না মরার নেয় পণ,
তবে মানুষরা কেন হেরে যাই,
কেন ভাবি সব শেষের আগেই শেষ।

শেষ সব গল্পেরই হয়, হবেই একদিন যবনিকা পাত।
তবু মানুষই পারে শেষ দৃশ্যটার সুন্দর রূপ দিতে।
যেদিন সবাই কাঁদবে, শুধু সে হাসবে।
অগাধ এক শান্তি, তৃপ্তি তার বুকে।
না পাওয়াতেও আছে যে সুখ,
সে কি নিজেকে শেষ করলে পাবে??

11. Sacrificed the most, Suffered the worst

A nation was born- divided and torn.

Nothing left to mourn.

Refugee has become the tag of millions.

Bengal and Punjab-

Who have contributed the most.

For the cause of independence,

For the cause of protecting their mother land,

For the cause of building a beautiful nation,

For the cause of identity and self determination.

Partition- A bolt from the blue, like nobody has the clue.

Separated into two-

A wound which was never healed.

Chapter12

বলা হয় পর্থম পের্ম কেউ ভুলতে পারে না।
আসলে কেউ শেষ পের্ম হওয়ার চেষ্টা কি করে?
পর্থম পের্মের আনন্দ হারিয়ে ফেলে সব,
কেউ বা ভুলতে গিয়ে মনে করে বেশি তাকে।
কেউ বা তাকে পেয়ে ভুলে যায় সব অভাব,
ভালো দেখলেও লাগে ভয়, কত কু ডাকে।
ভালবাসা মানে শুধু কি দেনা পাওনার হিসেব?
দূরে থেকেও তার ভালো চাওয়া কি নয়?
লোকে বলে পর্থম পের্ম ভোলা যায় না,
পের্ম তো চিরন্তন, যা শেষ অবিদ থাকে।
কাউকে হারিয়ে ফেলতে কে বা চায়।
যারা থাকার তারা কারন ছাড়া ও থাকে।
তাই নুড়ি পাথরের খোঁজে নিজেকে হারাই,
নিজে? সেই বা হিরের চেয়ে কম কি।
তাই ক্ষতি কি পরাণ ভরে আজ বেঁচে,
যা তোমার ই তা থাকবেই চিরদিন।

13. I, Me & Myself

I am what I am,
I have never regret.
I have cried, I have failed.
I am break free.
I behaved like stupid.
Have tasted failure.
Have been bullied several times.
But, have never stepped back,
I have never quit.
Have never afraid to fight.
Will rise from the ashes,
Will learn from everything.
I will rise from the heart break and trauma.
I will write my story till full stop.
I, who never regret-
One day I will be on top.

Chapter14

সেই কবে থেকে লিখতে বসেছি,
কবিতার বেশে মনের কথাগুলো।
দিয়েছি তাকে কত রূপ,
দিয়েছি কত ছান্দনিক আকার।
করোনার এই ভয়াল পরলয়,
কাড়ছে জানা অজানা হাজারো পরিচয়।
চারদিকে এত মৃতুয়্ভয়-
তবু আছে সাহস, আছে ভরসা।
শেষ থেকেই তো সব শুরু হয়।।
শেষ হয়েও কি সব হয় শেষ,
মানুষের মাঝে আজ ও এতো রাগ-বিদেব্ষ।
মানুষের সুখ মানুষ দেখে মানুষ ই বড় দুঃখী,
দুঃখ দেখে দুঃখী হলে ও মনে মনে হয় সুখী।
তাই আজ রাস্তা জুড়ে বল হরি হরিবোল,
পৃথিবীর এই গভীর অসুখে শুধু কান্নার রোল।
অনেয়র দুঃখে সুখী মানুষগুলো ও আজ কাঁদছে।
সবার শেষেও শেষমেশ কিছুই শেষ হয়নি।
আসলে সবার শেষে কিছু শেষ হয়না,
নতুন গল্পের শুরু সবার শেষ থেকেই হয়।।

15. Pain in the pen (Poetry on male's right)

As they say-
"No pain, no gain".
But here we will sing
All about the men.
We talk about human rights.
Feminism, Womens right & empowerment.
So many term, policy, committee for all of it.
But what about men's right??
What about male's human right??
Really??
Talking about it is so embrassing.
We males are born super human.
Or like the robot.
Who are as hard like rock.
As per bollywood
"Mard ko dard nehi hota".
For some we are made of stone.
Stone does not have pain.
Stone does not feel pain.
So as we.
We dont feel pain-
Neither for us, nor for any of us.

Sounds like stone hearted.

Is not it??

Still many question lies

Whether we are allowed to have pain?

Whether we have the right to our tears?

To cry loud,

To scream like none listening to us.

Alas!!

They neither listen, nor care to listen.

Crying man?? Its not a mainstream.

It will not get the milege, the trp

That needed to get in the news.

For some we are born criminal.

Some declare eve teaser, rapist, women abuser.

Before we can have a fare trial.

For them we enjoy a slight touch of women.

Intentionally or unintentionally

Irrespective of whose intention.

Irrespective of who needs an attention.

We celebrate womens day

Have seminar, paper presentation, workshop and many more.

Cards, whatsapp, facebook wishes.

Though there may be men's day

At the end of 'no shave november'

But how many people knows it

How many women remembers it.

How many organization organize seminar, workshop for it.

Forget it.

How many awareness camp is there on that day?

How many??

Just to tell the world-

Women are not always the victims,

The sufferer,

Not the only one who sacrifices.

Not the only one who face abuses-

Physical or mental.

Everyone in this world playing their role.

They came here to play on their own way.

From insects to human, everyone.

Equity, a key for better tomorrow.

The disease lies in the domination.

"Happiness of a family lies in the hand of a virtuous woman".

Is it-

A family consists of both-men & women.

Compromise and understanding-

Only what it takes

Only what it needs

For a family to be happy forever.

As they said-

"All starts with family and ends with family".

Rightly said.

All good and bad-

All took birth only in a family.

Nobody should be subject to abuse.

Slapping a woman is as immoral as slapping a man-
Be it in private or in public.
In fact we are too judgemental-
We judge people on the basis of dresses, color, food, habit.
Let there be a gender neutral law.
You are not guilty till you are proven guilty.
Irrespective of your sex.
Irrespective of the nature of the offenses.
Till then-
Pain will remain in the pen.

16. Hey Loser

Loser-

Is it just a mere term for calling someone?

or

It just synchronizes with bullying.

Or its just a word.

A word which will help us.

Help us??

Really?

How?

Yes, to chose between-

Either you down and drowned in depression

or wake up, start again and rise.

Just to find a right direction.

Just to find an excuse to rise and rise again.

Loser, I just take it as a compliment.

Yes, you heard it right.

Whenever someone calls me-

"HEY LOSER"

That means I am worth talking of.

That means I have not stopped trying.

Life is like a match-

Game is not over till the last ball bowled.

Till the final whistles blown.

Till the best shot was served.

Till someone finishes the touch line.

But if-

If what??

IF NOTHING HAPPENS

It will be not happened if you think it will not happen.

Till the final call-

You are never done.

When you can't inspire yourself,

How can you inspire others.

"Stop not till the goal is reached"

You know why Bruce made history-

He could have given up.

He could have drowned in the wilderness.

But he tried, tried and tried.

The only thing that matters.

Remember-

You refused to quit,

You deny the despair.

You are stronger than ever-

You just don't know it.

You don't know the power within.

Time has come to re discover,

Just outnumber all your fear.

You have all the power.

You don't know it, just don't know it.

17. Rejection

We hindus believed that word is param brambho,
For us word is as powerful as god.
Word spoken cannot be taken back-
Be it good or bad.
Be it blessings or curses.
Word can spear your heart like no other weapon.
Here is the catch-
Death may be the second scariest word,
First will remain rejection.
This word may be as haunted as hell.
From king to beggar, irrespective of its skin color.
Irrespective of its race and religion.
For someone, its a poison.
No scope for digestion.
But is it a poison?
There will be either acceptance or rejection.
In the absence of rejection life would have been stuck-
Stuck in the middle of yes or no.
More pathetic and brutal than we can think of.
Fear of Rejection-
Could not convert many feelings into beautiful ending.
Could not turn good citizen into candidature in elections.

Could not help an employee to get a better place or promotion-

Or towards a journey from an employee to entrepreneur.

Rejection is that word we cannot think beyond-

But is not something better than nothing.

You know rejection has so much to offer.

Rejection ensures a result-

May be you will not cherish the result you get after the rejection.

You will at least get the result.

Is it not better to face the adrenal than to wait for eternal.

Rejection ensures a move on-

To find something better.

To become better ;

for us or someone.

To enter into the next level.

Am I romanticizing rejection?

May be but one thing I am here to tell you.

Rejection let you know who you are,

Rejection let you know your real power.

Either you make it to create history

or

There is no other or.

There should not be any.

It is very easy to mark an end,

Death is eternal.

Let the good things come to you,

Don't make rejection as the barrier.
Your kingdom is waiting for its ruler,
Let the rejection become the reason of your redemption.

18. শুধু তোমার জন্য

আমি জানি না তুমি কোথায় আছো,
কেমন ই বা তুমি দেখতে।
তবু এই কবিতাটা-
শুধু তোমার জন্য, শুধু তোমার ই জন্য।
জানো খুব রোম্যান্টিক আমি,
কত না জানি স্বপ্ন বুনে রেখেছি।
এভাবে পর্পোস করবো, এই এই ফুল দেবো।
লিখবো হাজারো কবিতা তোমাকে নিয়ে।

ভাঙা গলাতেও গাইবো অনেক গান,
হাসলেও জানি শুনবে মন দিয়ে।
তোমার হাসির এক পশলা ঝলক,
উড়ে গেল সব মন খারাপের মেঘ।

ভাবছো, এত স্বপ্ন কি করে দেখি-
যেদিকে তাকাও হৃদয় ভাঙার গল্প।
অভাবে নাকি ভালবাসা ছেড়ে যায়,
ব্যথ্রতা দেখে পালানোর পথ খোঁজে।

পের্য়সী, তবে তুমি আমায় বলো-
স্বপ্ন ছাড়া বাঁচতে পারা কি যায়?
স্বপ্নতেই পর্থম তোমার সাথে দেখা,
স্বপ্ন বাস্তব হওয়ার অপেক্ষায়।
জমে আছে কত ক্ষোভ আর অভিমান,

জমাট বাঁধা বুকের মাঝের ক্ষত।

তুমি আসলে গল্প হবে অনেক,
হাতের মধেয় হাতটা খালি রেখো।

এই কবিতাটা তোমায় নিয়ে লেখা,
শুধু তোমার নামটা বসিয়ে নিও।

ততদিন থাকবো তোমার পর্তীক্ষায়-
শুধু তোমার জনয়, শুধু তোমার ই জনয়।

19. Circle of Hatred

People say everything starts with a family.

Everything starts in a family.

Yes, every good and bad things.

Respect and hatred.

Friendship and quarrel.

If no, then tell me-

How a child learned jealousy.

None is born criminal.

They learn it in the family,

They know it in their surroundings.

But how-

How a family carry the legacy of hatred.

Astonished?

No, I am not.

WE SEE IT EVERYWHERE.

It all starts with the member of a family-

Maternal or paternal is not relevant.

It all starts with the bitter experience-

While dealing with,

While talking with,

Irrespective of ethnicity, religion, caste, sex they have.

Even hatred for a stray.

Bitter experience of a person becomes the tradition.

Yes, tradition to hate someone.

Bitter experience then carries from father to son and so on.

A saplings become great banyan tree.

A bad person then started representing a whole community.

A bad person then become definition of a community.

So a judgemental person and a bitter experience.

Hatred is born in a clan.

A chain of hatred.

Now its up to us-

This younger generation.

Either we break this chain

Or lets carry this tradition of hatred.

20. Mental

The thing we have-
But we forget.
Forget to care,
Forget to nurture,
Forget to discuss,
Forget that it is our integral part.
Can you tell me?
Guess? Anything??
Yes, I am talking about mental health.
People find out easy to tag someone 'mental'.
Such tagging may question their mental health.
May be they are judgemental.
May be they have lost their path.
Lost the connection in the era of well connectivity, Broadband and 5G.
So many terms, so many invention-
Some of them new or old.
Some of them known or unknown.
In this modern world we have discovered many things.
But still-
Psychology is a mystry.
As they said- "A science without definition".
Rightly said.

Every human is different.

Still we talk less, act lesser-

About our mind.

Which may be screaming for help.

But we could not listen,

We don't want to listen.

You know ignorance is the best medicine.

It is, was, always.

Medical expenses are getting expensive day by day.

Price rise is everywhere with his bosom friends-

Corruption, War, Unemployment and many menaces.

Who will care for mind when body is at stake.

When still it is a dream,

To enjoy two quarter meal.

To have some sleep.

When mind is good all is good.

We could not see the mind.

But the mind is the master mind of every action.

Good things or worst.

Sounds like tongue twister.

Lets make it simple.

When the mind is strong and healthy,

Where the mind can fly break free,

We secure violence free future,

We ensure a society worthy to live.

21. FAME-US

Who don't wanna be famous?

None.

You, me, everyone.

Everyone wants to get recognized.

Not only from now,

But from the time immemorial.

We can find 'Yasho dehi' in the holy book Chandi.

"Give us fames".

It is the prayer for the ages,

Even from the sages.

This is the age of information technology.

We live in the social media,

We eat it, we drink it.

Thanks to covid,

We could not live without it..

Status, post, like, share, comment and many more.

We live here more than we live in the real.

Has not the social media become our silent companion?

Killing the fear of getting alone.

But is it?

Have not we stuck in the virtual world?

Where everybody needs attention,

In no time wants to become sensation,

Where everybody dreams to be famous,

Where any achievement make people jealous.

We are connected through devices but detached from heart.

Now we have friends in benefit.

For me good work gets you not only fame, but everything.

May be people forget or don't know the difference.

The difference between one day sensation and remembering

for millenials.

Fame is like the time,

Washed away.

We have it today, we have the today.

Tomorrow is unknown.

The balance between 'fame' and 'us'.

Will be there if you focus.

Any disbalance will make you unhappy,

You will be curdled by loneliness,

No reason will make you depressed.

Because You don't have you.

Like the term 'growth', 'development'.

Rome was not built on a day.

To live happy and meaningful-

The only thing that matters.

22. ENDANGERED

When the threat of extinction dance upon the head,
When life feels like very cheap.
Talking about endangered.
So many species gone, gone forever.
Heartless and careless when come together
Nothing will last.
But nothing last forever, everything has validity
But have you seen bestiality gone from animal??
It lies with him till its dead, till its extinguished.
It never gone before it gone
Human the best creation of God or
Or the tool of annihilation;
When humanity is at stake.
When humanity is looking like disappeared-
Before the human race gone.
Now who is endangered-
Human, humanity or humanity carrying human.

23. AGONY OF LAWYERS

Lawyers-

For some we are blood suckers.

Demands money here and there.

For some we are there to provide free service.

Asking fees is a crime.

Getting a loan is still a dream till-

till you have become senior,

or you have well paying client.

To show you have a bank balance to repay.

But still question lies-

Needs make you ask for loan.

Sometimes its become nightmare-

A ghost reality,

To ask her dad to marry his daughter.

Not so privilege like engineers, doctors or government servant-

None wants a lawyer son-in-law.

Specially if they are first generation lawyers.

Lawyers have 'L', so have a labour.

But later have social security.

They have many NGOS for their issue.

Various schemes, allowance, insurance from the government-

Both at center and state.

Though lawyers attend hearing for the people, for the government.

Hiding their pain which speaks for itself.

Still their agony is unheard-

By the people, by the Government, by the temple of Justices.

Covid & lockdown made it worst.

When there is no infrastructure in the court-

Work from home is as illusory as golden bowl.

The agony of the first generation lawyers-

Higher than you can imagine.

More internship, opportunities if not come to them-

None will join in future.

No young star will come to showcase their talent.

Remember-

Everyone needs a lawyer.

Be it I.T company, start up or private firm-

Society needs brother-in-arm.

lawyers are none other than soldiers.

They fought in the battle field,

We battle in the every field,

Even battle for them.

As the social engineer we build bridges-

To connect people with justice.

As the social doctor we try to cure all the social evils.

Lawyers-

When there is no way,

There is a clear dead end.
We find the way.
We will find the way.
Today, tomorrow and always.

24. Make Life Meaningful

Life does not mean,
It will have life in it.
Life may not be lively as it looks like.
Social media is illuson.
It mislead, it deceives.
May be for that rich persons have sleepless night.
There is no perfect life.
But life does become perfect-
When people never give up,
When people starts walking to become worthy.
Worthy for them, for the society.
When people strive to learn everyday
When people starts finding purpose of its life.
Learning everyday in life
Learning make life meaningful.

25. BARRIER

Barrier

What do we mean by it

A wall or something stops us

Which stops us.

Which stay between us and our destination

A boundary- which needs to be crossed.

Or may need to jumped over.

But who made boundaries?

We the human.

We made wall, boundaries.

Between people or

Builtit in our mind

Which we dont want to get crossed-

By us or by someone.

Becuse they love to stay away

But why are they fleeing away and from whom

From people or from their soul

To live in the boundaries

Set by them for them.

They neither know nor want to know

They are infinite, they come from infinite

Nothing can stop them except them.

It is them, it is them, it is them

Chapter26

ভালবাসা কি সেটা বুঝেছি মা কে দেখে,
যে আমায় জন্ম দিয়েছে, সহয় করেছে অনেক কষ্ট।
করতে হয়েছে অনেক কিছুর তয্াগ-
সুখ, সব্াচ্ছন্দয্, আরাম, কেরিয়ার
না জানি আরো কত কি।
ঠিক আমার দেশের মত।
যাকে ক্ষতবিক্ষত করে দিয়েছিল র্যাডক্লিফ লাইন।
এক মা ভাগ হয়ে গেল তিন ভাগে।
কিন্তু লড়াই এখনো থামে নি, আরো জোরদার হয়েছে।
জাতি, ধ্মর, ব্ণর, রং, ভাষা;
কখন ও বা খাদয্াভয্াস, এমনকি চোখের গড়ন ও বেশভূষা।
মায়ের বুকের পাঁজর আজ ছিন্নভিন্ন, রক্তাক্ত।
ওরে, আর কত রক্ত ঝরলে তোরা থামবি।
আর কত মা কোল শূনয্ দেখে বিলাপ করবে।
চল না, এই দেশের বুকে সব্গর নামিয়ে আনি।
মন খুলেই বল একবার-
ভালোবাসি এই দেশ কে।

27. MY DEAR JAGANNATH

This poetry is only for you-
My life, my everything;
Which revolves around you.
Like this galaxy, this jagat.
Jagannath-Lord of this universe.
My guru, my best friend.
My friend, philosopher and guide.
My everything, my breathe, my body-
I surrender my all to thee.
When there was none,
If there will be none-
To stand for me, before me.
I know you will be there.
Like everytime you were there.
When my shadow leave me, you were there.
You were there when I was not born,
You were there when there was no creation.
You will be there when I will left to your heavenly abode.
This is only for you,
My poetry, my spirituality, my austerity.
I devote all I have.
But what I have.

When I was born I had nothing but this body
That too given by my parents.
When I will leave I will have nothing,
Forget my earnings, I will even leave my body.
But your teaching may never leave me.
Serve jeeva means serve you.
"ALL ROAD LEADS TO THEE"
ALL GLORY LEADS TO THEE
ALL WORSHIP LEADS TO THEE.
Oh gracious!
Oh Lord!
We bow down to thee.

28. THE ONLY THING THAT IS FREE

Though I belong to 90's but when I heard this word-
"Free".
I got two thoughts-
One dialogue from 3 idiot movies.
"Farhan will marry your sister for free"
That means without dowry.
Though marriage may be the only thing,
That comes with a fee to pay.
You have to pay for the lifetime.
Another is jio telecomes free internet service in 2016.
Though when I was kid I still remember-
Many vendors offer buy one get one free.
On clothes, grocery, accessories.
Free sweets on Poila Baisakh(Bengali new year)
or Akshay Tritiya.
But every things come with a price-
Though it may hide, adjusted or by lowering the margin,
the margin of profit, gain or interest.
Nothing is free here.
Water, air, land, sky, fire- nothing.
And all those feelings, emotion-
You need to invest something to maintain.

You know what I mean.

For the noble work, you need to invest money.

From your savings, earnings, funding whatsoever.

Love someone of our choices still unimaginable.

Even dream has many cost.

You need to work hard.

Volunteering??

That can be done for either experience or exposure.

But, but-

There is one thing,

may be the only thing.

Human is prawn to it.

Human learn it from childhood.

To hate someone-

For its caste, color, creed, language, religion;

or for no reason,

or for an excuse.

Now you may ask me how?

Hatred lands you in jail.

No, not right.

Showcasing hatred does that.

But not every time.

Humans don't need talent.

They can hate you in heart.

They can hate you even in your presence,

You just don't know it.

The only thing that can be exploited easily,

The only thing unmasked easily.
It is free, free and free.

29. TROLL

This world is full of troll-
They are jealous, they are unhappy.
They cant see someone going ahead;
Fulfilling his aim, living his dream.
Are they hopeless, finding no clue?
About their life, about the purpose.
But life needs happiness-
Dimnishing their own capacity by demeaning others.
Are they not demeaning themselves.
Those clueless don't know time is cruel.
They don't know time is money.
They don't know demean is a demon.
Wasting instead of focussing.
On themselves.
To know how good they are,
To know how much they have the capacity.
To build something good, something worthy.
Maybe they need help,
Asking in harsh manner.
But they should know,
About the troll.
Troll is like a ladder.
Either they use it to reach the top,

or they quit by jumping off.
Like I have said quit is not the solution,
Like the troll.
It never was, never will be.

30. A BENGALI SUPERHERO

From my childhood to today,

I love comics.

Yes till today.

I will read it in future with my future..

But I used to ask my grandmother,

When I was a little one.

When a bengali super hero will arrive.

Like the Shaaktiman.

Which comes every sunday in DD one.

When I will meet.

One day my father took me to meet someone,

It was a lunch invitation.

"GOOPY GAYEN"

Who got three boon from king of ghosts.

"So you have identified me, the cute little pie"

"Meet with the bengalis first super hero" my father said

It was a fanboy moment, dream comes true.

Goopy and bagha- the ideal bengali superheros.

Who got what every bengali wants to have.

To have the food whatever,

To travel anywhere,

To being a flawless musician.

By this power they have stopped the war,
The war between halla and shundi.
They have overthrown the autocrat from Diamond province.
They have defeated the black magician.
They don't have muscular body to flaunt for-
Just like you and me.
Having a dream to change the world.
To make this world better place-
For living a wonderful life.
I was very young then,
when I met Goopy gayen in person,
But could not meet Bagha Bayen.
They are the first bengali Super hero.
Having simplicity now a days-
In this world of traitors and liars;
Nothing but a superpower.

Chapter31

আমাদের ভবিষ্যত পরজন্ম অন্ধকারে থাকলে,
আমাদের ভবিষ্যত কে গরাস করবে কাজল কালো অন্ধকার।
কাল নিজেকে বাঁচাতে চাইলে আজ কে দিশা দেখাতে হবে,
পাশে দাঁড়িয়ে থাকতে হবে।

আমাদের ভবিষ্যত যাদের হাতে,
শক্ত করতে হবে তাদের কচি হাতগুলো।
আমাদের হাতে যে বর্তমান আছে তা বর্তমানে নষ্ট করলে,
ভবিষ্যতের হাতে থাকা বর্তমান হয়ে যাবে মূল্যহীন।
ওদের চোখে আছে অনেক সবপ্ন,
নতুন কিছু করার জন্য আছে উদয়ম, আছে সাহস।
দিশার অভাবে আশাহীন হয়ে করে ফেলে সব নষ্ট,
মন খুলে তবু হাসতে জানে আসুক যতই কষ্ট।
আজকের চারাগাছগুলো কাল হয়ে উঠবে বট,
যদি একটু দিশা দেখাই, ধরিয়ে দি সব ভুল।
মরার কথা ভুলে আনন্দে হয়ে ওঠ মশগুল।
আমরা যা যা পাইনি তা তোদের উজার করে দেব,
এভাবেই না হয় সুন্দর এক সমাজ গড়ে নেব।
এইভাবে আমি সবপ্ন দেখি, হই না যতই শূন্য।
ওদের জন্য না করলে জীবন হবে না পূর্ণ।
যতদিন পূর্ণ হবে না সবপ্ন বারবার ফিরে আসবো,

নেতাজির হাঁটা পথটা ধরে ভারতকে ভালবাসবো।

32. ADVOCATING DOCTORS

Doctors-

A noble profession with long and never ending schedule.

A noble profession which forget to eat, sleep and repeat.

A noble profession which are judged here and there,

Even sometimes for nothing;

Even sometimes it was not their fault.

We complain but visits them-

Only they can save our lives.

Who said they are not corrupt?

But they are not the only one who corrupts.

In fact, it is not them-

It is the system,

It is the acceptance of that system,

It is that misunderstanding,

It is not understanding them,

As we never understood each other.

As there is a huge wall between us separated,

A huge gap fulfilled by all the middleman.

Many people still cannot afford word class health care,

Many could not pay the fees to become a doctor.

Is it just a fees?

Even whole family cannot even dreamt of making this much
money.

Forget politics, they had to fight with zero infrastructure.

Blaming is an easy game,

Doctor, patient whoever we are.

Lets fight for our right to health.

Lets secure our health,

For us, for doctors.

33. Leave it or Live it

You don't have a choice!!
Who said that?
Who said it to whom?
If it has been said between two or more,
That you don't have a choice;
One must have known-
That always there was a choice.
That always there is a choice.
A choice to choose for-
Make it or break it.
Leave the dream or live it.
Leave the race or be the race
Leaving is very easy-
I know you will make it.
I know you can do it.
YES, YOU.
The most courageous and strongest

34. Grant me Leave

Like everyone in this world,
I want to get vanished for one day.
Oh dear, Oh Lord!!
I feel I need rest.
I feel I need a long sleep.
To spend some days without worrying,
A day without any panic attack,
A day without depression.
Sound sleep without bed bugs bite,
Oh Lord! Grant me leave for a day.
For atleast one day.
Let me breathe some fresh air.
One day, that's what I need.
To fix all the issues I have.
To fix the life once again,
Grant me one day of leave,
My leave of absense

35. A Needle of Pain

Today I asked a phlebotomists to come home;
For my blood test,
To know and check about my health.
I had experience of giving blood for a cause.
Still I got panicked!!!
What will happen to me?
When that needle will enter into my vein-
I will be under tremendous pain.
What will happen, what will happen?
Are you smiling?
You should because I have caused it.
All though that phlebotomist is known to me for years.
I have become fool enough after the hit of covid-19.
Lockdown not only ruined,
but made my life restless in the true sense or other;
Restless or rest less.
I got panicked here and there.
Who don't afraid of ghost or anything,
but got afraid of a 2 inch needle.
Two inch needle penetration got over me.
Forget that life gives more pain than a needle.
Forget that every pain makes us-
Stronger than ever.

I forget that, I really forget that.

Chapter36

বন্ধুত্ব-একটা গভীর শব্দের নাম।
যে নিজে একটি সম্পর্ক,
কিন্তু সব সম্পর্ক সে বিনা নিস্তেজ।
যাকে দরকার প্রতিটি সম্পর্কের গভীরে।
সে থাকলে প্রতিটি সম্পর্ক হয়ে ওঠে আরো গাঢ়।
একটা বন্ধু সব সময়েই প্রয়োজন।
সব সময় পাশে থাকার নামই তো বন্ধুত্ব।
বন্ধুত্ব মানে হাত বাড়ালেই যাকে পাওয়া যাবে।
শীত, গ্রীষ্ম কিংবা বর্ষরা-
বন্ধু মানে একটু আশা আর অনেকটা ভরসা।
বন্ধুত্ব মানে মন আর মুখ এক।
যে মুখে না, কাজেও সে বন্ধু।
যে শুধু বিপদে না, সুখে ও পাশে চাইবে।
ব্যথ্রতার কানাগলি পেরিয়ে যখন সাফল্য আসবে,
বেকারত্ব পেরিয়ে যখন আসবে কাজের সুযোগ।
বন্ধু তখন হয়ে ওঠে না অচেনা।
বন্ধুকে সারাক্ষণ করতে হয় না ফোন, মেসেজ-
সে যেখানেই থাকুক,
সে ঠিক বুঝিয়ে দেয়,
সে ছিল, সে আছে।
যে থাকতে আসে, সে থেকেই যায়।
থাকার কারণ নিজেই খুঁজে নেয়।

37. A short one

This story is about the short one,
For the world they are dwarf.
For the world they are insignificant.
No attention for them.
No separate news coverage.
But it is also their world,
They have their own world.
They are not the most eligible bachelors in the town.
Who will marry those 'liliputs'?
When it is the crime for having the height-
The height of lower than average.
Are they normal??
Do we treat them normal?
Look at them
Like an alien came
Or they are the beast
Or the worst body human can have.
But it is neither fault nor a sin.
It is the hormone.
We read it in our text book,
Taught every year in the class room.
Still we don't fail to bully.
Is it not a devil's pleasure.

In this era of kali(demon),

We have all become devil personified.

None represent them, they represent none.

Do we consider them as human?

I believe in the magic of creator,

They will rise, rise on their own;

To reach a height-

None have ever have,

None have ever thought of

38. A PROUD INDIE

Proud to be an Indian-
Yes, we wrote it on red letter day.
We wrote in the social media here and there.
But still we hesitate to buy Indian products.
Still we think out of a colonial belief,
Indian product is worst and cheap.
Those puppies are not an object or product,
Cutest thing you can ever see.
They can not be thrown like an useless toy,
They love you more than you.
They live and die for you,
They want love and care,like every creature.
If you can not find love and life on strays-
Still searching for a foreign breed,
You think you are buying lively object,
But believe me they are not an object you can buy.
You can not, you should not.
You can't cast your caste on them-
Some superior, some untouchable.
Love them as they are-
From a proud Indian,
Who adopted indie pup.

39. Zero

Everything starts with zero,
Everyome starts from zero,
But everyone hates zero.
Why not, it has no value.
Who wants to be valueless?
None wants a valueless.
But here is the catch.
What is value and what has less value.
Success depend on that person's perspective.
For someone, you may be a big zero-
For your look or for your height,
Earning less means no respect.
But it is them, what do you think?
Do you value yourself?
Do you know yourself?
Do you think you are trying?
Do you think you are growing?
Do you think you have not quit or have you?
Your answer decides what you are.
Life is the story of zero's way of motion-
Either you make it suffix or prefix.
When you stops you,
When you blocks your growth,

When you rely too much on someone;about you
You become zero-for you and others.

40. Why I love Germany

I have never been to Germany.

But still I love this country.

For me it is a country of dream.

I had a Jersey of Germany football team.

Lahm, Ballack, Close was my favourite Euro cup star.

Gerd Muller came to Howrah along with its U23 team,

The youth team of Bayern Munich.

Thomas Muller and Holger was in that youth team.

Baycrn Munich, my favourite club team was then.

Oliver Kahn, the great wall.

Who played his farewell match against my beloved Mohun
Bagan.

In 2008, Bayern ruled the Europe that year.

Oliver Kahn played in front of 1,20,000 people.

But still you may ask why not U.S or U.K?

Specially if you are an Indian,

You will definitely feel.

Germay suffered the partition like India.

But Germans could break the wall.

The wall of division, difference and disdain.

Or we can say the wall of hatred.

As a student of Howrah Vivekananda Institution-

I heard the name of Max Muller,

The great German philosopher.

There is a Max Muller Bhawan in Kolkata.

In my childhood I used to read his book.

Specially his communication with Swami Vivekananda.

History was always my favourite subject.

I still remember those days, when I was in class eight.

At that time Bengal was ruled by communists.

So Karl Marx was well known from primary school.

So as Bishmark, Hegel, Kant.

Subhas Chandra Bose, a bengali, India's super hero.

Who got help from Germans for the fight for our independence.

Satyendra Nath Bose, a bengali, inspiration for the scientists.

Bose-Einstein theory is still relevant to decode many mysteries,

The mystery of this universe.

Einstein even met Rabindranath Tagore in 1930-31.

Who was the first Asian noble laureate.

Germany means comeback against odd,

Germany means history, pride and glory,

Germany means India's trusted friend.

Germany which fight back against nazi rule.

You said fighting spirit, never give it up-

I heard Germany, I heard Germany.

41. What you want? (To all the readers)

Lets make it simple,

or just in a poetic manner.

It is my question-

Question, no no.

My humble prayers.

Just to know what you want.

100+ days gone,

Thirsts for the good work,

Hunger to give you good content.

Being a lawyer and lawet-

Law will be there always.

But what types of law blog you want-

You want to see, read and experiment.

Legislative review or research on issues.

No option for less.

Provide me more.

As I say more to come.

Lawet is law, poetry, you and me.

Here 'you' means more to me.

More to offer for you.

Law, religion, sports, social issues.

Poetry will be there to complete.

Just let me know in the comments-
What you want.
We can have live conversations.
To know your wish.
At your service-
Lawet, for you always.

Chapter42

আমরা মানুষ রা অভিনয় করি,

পরতিনিয়ত করে চলি নাটক,

এই পৃথিবীর নাটয্শালায়-

বিস্মৃতি বা বিস্মৃত হওয়ার।

বলি সব কিছুই ভুলে গেছি।

আসলে কিছুই ভুলি নি,

আসলে মনের গভীরে সযত্নেই করি লালন পালন।

ভুলতে পারি না কিছু অচেনা মানুষকে,

যারা অচেনা হয়েও না জানি কত চেনা।

সাথে থেকেছে হাত শক্ত করে।

ভুলতে পারিনি সেই চেনা মানুষ গুলো কে ও।

আসলে এটা বুঝতে পারি নি,

বুঝতে পারি নি তাদের কোনটা আমার চেনা-

মুখ না তাদের মুখোশ?

বন্ধুর বিপদ দেখলেই যেটা খসে পড়ে।

বন্ধুর বিপদে বন্ধু তলিয়ে যায় বিস্মৃতির অতল গহব্বরে।

আমার স্মৃতিশক্তি টা আবার একটু বেশীই সতেজ।

পের্রকের ছোটো খাটো জিনিস ও ভুলি না।

সে সাহাযয্ হোক বা দূবরয্বহার।

বদলা??

না না।

বদলা তো তাদের গুরুতব্ বাড়িয়ে দেবে।
তার চেয়ে ও বেশী গুরুতব্পূণর সব্য়ংসম্পূণর হয়ে ওঠা।
নিজের লক্ষে অবিচল এক সব্য়ংসিদ্ধ।
পর্শংসা বা তিরস্কার যার ভিত কাঁপাতে পারে না।
হয়ে ওঠে গীতায় ব্ণিরত সেই আদ্শর পুরুষ।।

43. Simple Rule of Love

Love- is it too simple or complicated?
Is it just a feelings of something euphoric?
What can be the simple rule of love?
Rules- for love or being loved.
What do you mean by love?
Is it just a mere relationship between opposite sex?
Is it rely upon opposite gender?
Is it depends on same religion, language, caste?
Is there separate language of love?
Love has become agreement- is not it?
With so much terms, conditions and clauses.
Look at the animals-
They love each other.
They love humans.
Human has various language,
Still they understand the language.
For them love is the language.
For them love is trust.
For them love don't have requisite, but it is.
We have so many language to understand,
but we misunderstood;
May be this is why human lives longer
It took decades for them,

to understand love;
but still they can't.
They can not recognize the simple rule of love,
They don't live and let live.

Chapter44

এই কবিতা টা বন্ধুদের জন্য উ?স্গর করেছি,
আর উ?স্গর করেছি নিজের প্রতি।
আমরা একদিন একসাথে শুরু করেছিলাম সেই যাত্রা।
সেই যাত্রা শুরু হয়েছিল স্কুল ও কলেজ থেকে।
আজ একসাথে নেই, অনেকে সাথে নেই।
অনেকে থেকে ও নেই, অনেক কে চেয়ে ও নেই।
তবু একটা জিনিসে আমরা সবাই আছি-
লক্ষ্যর লক্ষ্যভেদে চলেছি এগিয়ে।
এই কবিতা টা লিখবো সেই কবে থেকে ভাবছি।
আজ লিখেই ফেললাম।
অনেকের নাম এই কবিতাতে নথিভুক্ত করবো ভেবেছিলাম।
তারা অনেকেই আজ অনেক দূরে-
অহংকারের নৌকায় অপমানের দাঁড় বেয়ে চলে গেছে তারা।
তারা হয়তো বিভিন্ন ভাবে সফল বা সফলতার পথে।
বা তারা যেখানেই থাকুক;
শুরু টা যখন একসাথে হয়েছে শেষ টা এক ভাবে হোক।
একদিন সবাই সফল হবো-
নিজের ভাবে, নিজের মত করে।

45. In the middle of something

Remember this phrase?
'In the middle of something'.
Max Payne 2, Second Chapter.
By the way Its a poetry afterall.
Not marketing, but sharing that memory.
Remember when we used to talk in the class.
Which interrupt the middle of something,
Which we find boring, some lectures!!
Is not it the art we human have mastered.
The art of leaving,
In the middle of something.
What! This phrase!
YES!!!!!
You do not believe me.
Let's find out.
We leave love while treating it like a casual,
We leave our cute helpless pet,
We leave our parents,
We leave our hope,
We leave our hardwork,
Whatever may be the reason.
But we leave them,

In the middle of something.

Chapter46

মহালয়ার ভোর, রেডিয়ো তে বেজে উঠলো মহিষাসুরমর্দিনী।
পূবের আকাশে উদিত রবি পর্কৃতি কে রঙিন করে তুলছে।
টের্ন লাইনের পাশের কাশফুলগুলো আনন্দে দোদুলয্মান;
মা যে আসছে।

চন্ডীস্তব শুনতেই কাঁচাঘুম ভেঙে উঠে পড়ে কচিকাঁচা থেকে
বয়স্করা।

তথ্যপর্যুক্তি থেকে কোনো বোরিং ডেস্কজব-
রাতজাগা ভোরের পাখিগুলো ও আজ বেশি করে জেগে।
কিসের এক উত্তেজনা পর্তিটি লোমকূপকে উদ্দীপ্ত করে
তুলেছে-
মা আসছে।

মন হোক বা দেহ, হাজারো ভিন্নতা থেকে রেডিয়ো;
সারা বছরের ধুলো, নোংরা যতই জমুক-
জমা হোক যত মন খারাপের রাত।

মা যে আমার সবার দুঃখ বোঝে,
মায়ের আমার দশ দশটি হাত।

দুগরা আসলে পর্তিটি মেয়ের গল্প, দশভুজা হয়ে দশদিকে যার
নজর।

দুগরা আসলে আশর্যের এক নাম-
আশর্য দিয়ে নিজের নেইকো আরাম।
হতাশার মাঝে আশার এক আলো;

মা আসছে, সবার করবে ভালো।

Chapter47

অনেকদিন বাদে লিখতে বসলাম,

কবিতার খাতা টা ঝেড়ে,

পাতা গুলো উল্টাতে লাগলাম।

যে পাতা গুলো ভর্তির হয়ে গেছে আর যেগুলো ভর্তির করতে বাকি।

কবিতা যে শুধু শুরু হয়, নেই তার পরিসমাপ্তি।

কিছু কবিতা অপূর্ণর হয়েও পূর্ণর, কিছু পূর্ণর হয়েও অসমাপ্ত থেকে যায়।

তাই নিরুপায় হয়েই উপায় করলাম আজ, অনুভূতি গুলো পাক কবিতার সাজ

আমি তখনো ছিলাম যখন তুমি চিনতে না এই শহর,ছিল না অত ফেসবুকের ধুম।

ছিল শুধু ভিজিএ কয্যামেরা, মানুষ হত না স্মার্টর ফোনে গুম।

ছিলাম পর্থম থেকেই, যখন তোমার পর্বেশ হয়নে এই অপার্থিরব দুনিয়াতে।

তবু দিতে পারি নি ফাস্টর লাইক বা কমেন্ট।

তবু ছিলাম আমি পাশেই, কিমি পাঁচেক দুর হয়তো হবে।

ডাকলেই পেতে হয়তো সাড়া, একটু খুঁজলে ই পেয়ে হয়তো যেতে।

ছিলাম ছয় নমব্রে, বন্ধু তালিকা যদি তুমি ঘাৎটলে।

দিনের শেষে ছটা লাইক হলেও, আমার লাইক টা খেয়াল কই বা করলে।

আসতে আসতে তালিকা হলো দীঘর, 500 লাইকে হারিয়ে গেলাম তাই-

ভালোবাসা তার ভালোর জন্যে বাঁচা, চিরদিন যার হাসি দেখতে চাই।

48. Insecurity

It all starts with a wound,
That is so fatal and haunting.
Like everyday its becoming worse.
Those nightmare keeps haunting back,
Even if there is nothing left-
To lose, to gain.
Even if it will never happen in future,
But the gravity of the wound makes it difficult.
To live in the present, to see the clear future.
But they cannot see, They live in the history.
These all brings the insecurity-
Insecurity of losing everything.
Losing its own identity, language and religion.
Losing its culture and many more, upon whom we fear.
Many has lost its dear from its near.
But we will fight back.
We will get over from the trauma.
We will have a future like a blue sky.
Only when we open the wounds for healing.
Have you checked the word 'Insecurity'.
It is the lock, it is the key.
When none will instill the fear,
When someone will wipe your tear.

When none will live in the past,

When none will exploit the trust.

When all the insecurity will cease,

There will be peace, peace and peace

49. My Elder sister

This poetry is for you,

Not for I am an emotional person you can ever see or

Today we are celebrating Rakhi.

It was my long standing dream,

It was my decade long wish.

But no word was enough to express my feelings.

Still no word can express it.

But I will fulfill my decade long wish.

Let me give a try.

You have been like a big banyan tree-

Who protects me from every odd.

You never let me worry about anything.

You fulfill my every wish.

Even those wish I hardly know.

Some of them even unknown to me.

But nothing can be hidden from you.

Like a mother,

Mother you are.

Thanks for everything.

50. Long Live the Liver

I have romanticised my blood test,
I have romanticised such other pain,
I have romanticised death.
Now let me romanticise my liver pain.
If you have read my 'L' story in Lawet,
You have definitely know how I love the 'L'.
L stands for Long, L stands for live.
If you want to live long,
You can not deny the liver.
We remember every simple thing;
even some complex formula.
Life itself has become very complicated.
But health is not that complex,
that is 'we'-
We make it complicated.
We forget us, as we forget our liver.
I have stated about live long, but-
If you want long life,
If you want to reign in the kingdom of food,
If you want to eat more, eat less now.
Make liver your best friend.
Liver- never harm it ever.

www.ingramcontent.com/pod-product-compliance
Lightning Source LLC
Chambersburg PA
CBHW061352160726
47995CB00001B/282